ADOPTION IS BOTH

BY ELENA S HALL

First Edition, October 2021

ISBN: 978-0-578-30621-6

Published by Elena S Hall
Printed and distributed through Kindle Direct Publishing

Illustrated by Lara Norris,
illustrations are her own and included in the copyright of this work

Editing and layout by Elena S Hall

Special thank you to Jonathan Jordan with Wordrobe Media

ADOPTION IS BOTH

for my sister

I was adopted,

I am an adoptee.

I can be happy, light, and carefree.

Adoption is happy and adoption is sad.
It can make my heart hurt
or make it feel glad.

There are days I miss people and have lots of questions.

There are other days I want to sing and dance about my family connections.

Adoption made my family and
I am an adoptee.

That is one thing that makes me, me!

My adoption is mine and my story is my own.

It's okay for some of my story
to be unknown.

It is okay to talk, or keep my story inside.

If I want to share, I can decide.

Adoptees are strong,

and carry a lot!

We can be teachers, actors, or astronauts!

Adoption may feel like a messy storm.

Adoption may feel so fun and warm.

If adoption is both happy and sad...

then it's okay to feel both glad AND mad.

Adoption is both – pink and blue!

Pink and Blue!

Both are true.

Made in United States
Orlando, FL
24 August 2023